31 Days of WINNING
WOMEN'S DEVOTIONAL & PRAYER JOURNAL

Jennifer L. Carner

JT Publishing House
www.jtpublishinghouse.com

Copyright © 2019 by Jennifer L. Carner

Published by JT Publishing Spartanburg, South Carolina
www.jtpublishinghouse.com

No part of this publication may be reproduced, stored in a retrieval system, or transmitted in any form or by any means, electronic, mechanical photocopying, recording, scanning, or otherwise, except as permitted under Section 107 or 108 of the1976 United States Copyright Act, without either the prior written permission of the author or authorization through payment of the appropriate per-copy fee to the Copyright Clearance Center, Inc. 222 Rosewood Drive, Danvers, MA 01923, 978-750-8400, fax 978-646-8600, or on the Web at www.copyright.com. Requests to the author for permission should be addressed to the Permissions Department, Jennifer L. Carner.

Limit of Liability / Disclaimer: The advice and strategies contained herein may not be suitable for your situation. You should consult with a professional where appropriate. Neither the Publisher nor the Author shall be liable for any loss of profit or any other commercial damages, including but not limited to special, incidental, consequential, or other damages.

Readers should be aware that Internet websites offered as citations and/or sources for further information may have changed or disappeared between the time this was written and when it is read. All rights reserved.

Scriptures taken from the Holy Bible, New International Version®, NIV®. Copyright © 1973, 1978, 1984, 2011 by Biblica, Inc.™ Used by permission of Zondervan. All rights reserved worldwide. www.zondervan.com The "NIV" and "New International Version" are trademarks registered in the United States Patent and Trademark Office by Biblica, Inc.™

Scripture taken from the New King James Version®.
Copyright © 1982 by Thomas Nelson. Used by permission. All rights reserved.

JT Publishing House books and products are available through most bookstores. To contact JT Publishing House, visit www.jtpublishinghouse.com.

Carner, Jennifer L.
31 days of winning: women's devotional & prayer journal/ Jennifer L. Carner.
South Carolina: JT Publishing House, 2019.

ISBN 978-1-7341793-0-9 (paperback) – ISBN 978-1-7341793-1-6 (ebook)
Library of Congress Cataloging-in-Publication Data: 2019916629
http://lccn.loc.gov/ 2019916629

Printed in the United States of America
10 9 8 7 6 5 4 3 2 1

Dedication

*For my parents, John and Brenda Carner.
Your courage enables me to soar.*

Contents

Introduction	9
Preface	11
The Power of Rest	13
Balance	17
Peace	21
Happiness	25
Focus	29
Safety	33
Freedom from Worry	37
Time Management	41
Reaching Out	45

Contents

Moving Forward	49
Weakness is Strength	53
Speak Life	57
Have Faith	61
Grow	65
Stay Alert	69
Patience	73
Hope	77
Look Up!	81
Insecure	85
Feed Your Spirit	89
Silence	93
Remember Who You Are	97
Seek Wisdom	101
Stay Away from Negativity	105
Joy	109
Trust	113
Refill Please	117
Fuel Yor Fight	121
Be Amazing	125
About the Author	129

Introduction

When you give so much, and exert so much energy to thrive, it becomes vitally important that you harness the power of your inner warrior.

Winning is not reserved for people who are famous, powerful, or perfect. Winning is what happens when we are mindful, centered, faith-filled, and whole.

Reflecting on the scriptures to achieve mindfulness and a centered self, opens us up to unfathomable peace.

This small devotional and journal will help you embrace a healthy headspace for winning. You will learn to embrace your own inner strength. Within

Introduction

these pages, special words of hope, are waiting for you. God wants you to grasp and be grasped by peace and joy.

May God's Word fill your heart and your mind. The work that has begun in your life, will be completed.

Let's win together!

Riches and honor come from you, and you rule over all. In your hand are power and might; and it is in your hand to make great and to give strength to all.
— 1 Chronicles 29:12 NRSV

Preface

It's not always easy to maintain your balance when hard things happen. At one of the most difficult times in my life, I could not be comforted.

I prayed, meditated, and attended worship regularly, but I could not find peace, so I wrote.

These devotional musings and exercises were the results of my rumination and resolve to win amid extreme personal turmoil.

It is my prayer that by completing this exercise, the exercise of rebuilding your strength when you have no strength left, that you will rise above any hard thing and become your highest self.

Preface

Each devotional thought is accompanied by a reflection section and an action section.

As I navigated my most challenging seasons of life and leadership, I read these thoughts and wrote a reflection about how the thought resonated with me and awakened my consciousness.

The action section is comprised of ways in which I could put what I received from the devotional thoughts into practice.

It is my prayer that these exercises will lift your heart and your head, as they lifted mine.

The Power of Rest

Know the value of rest and centering. Rest is not an option. It's a necessity!

How are you planning moments for rest today?

Rest helps you establish boundaries for your day.

Rest ensures that you have margin in your day for centering your thoughts. Rest has immeasurable health benefits.

Plan your rest to establish balance in your life today.

Reflection

Action

"It is a sabbath of complete rest to you, and you shall deny yourselves; it is a statute forever."
Leviticus 16:31

31 Days of Winning

Balance

Take time to live in the moment.

We live thinking too much about tomorrow, and we spend entirely too much time thinking and worrying about what we cannot change.

Live in the moment.

Enjoy the fruit of your labor.

Take long walks and sit in the shade.

You've earned it.

31 Days of Winning

Reflection

_____
_____
_____
_____
_____
_____
_____
_____
_____
_____
_____
_____
_____

Action

_____
_____
_____
_____
_____
_____
_____
_____
_____
_____
_____
_____

Balance

"And on the seventh day God finished the work that he had done, and he rested on the seventh day from all the work that he had done."
Genesis 2:2

31 Days of Winning

Peace

No more sleepless nights. Fear does not live here.

Whether you are single, married, searching, or satisfied, God keeps us safe.

Worry has no place in the life of the winning woman.

God protects, leads, guides, and fortifies us. God wants us to have peace.

Embrace yours today.

31 Days of Winning

Reflection

Action

Peace

"I will both lie down and sleep in peace; for you alone, O Lord, make me lie down in safety."
Psalm 4:8

31 Days of Winning

Happiness

Happiness is a choice.

We can allow our anxieties and our worries to win, or we can choose to win.

Happiness comes from knowing that God is with you and God cares for you.

Stop giving up valuable headspace to the opinions, thoughts, and expectations of others.

Think about the good things that are happening in your life and then, you'll be happy.

31 Days of Winning

Reflection

_____
_____
_____
_____
_____
_____
_____
_____
_____
_____
_____
_____

Action

_____
_____
_____
_____
_____
_____
_____
_____
_____
_____
_____
_____

Happiness

"Now rise up, O Lord God, and go to your resting place, you and the ark of your might. Let your priests, O Lord God, be clothed with salvation, and let your faithful rejoice in your goodness."
2 Chronicles 6:41

31 Days of Winning

Focus

Prioritize.

The potential to accumulate wealth and status will always be there, but family, friends, and opportunities to enjoy them will not.

You're a winning woman, that means you are probably busy.

Make time for the people who matter. Schedule family time and time for fun regularly.

It will help you stay balanced and focused in the long run.

Reflection

Action

Focus

> *"Sweet is the sleep of laborers, whether they eat little or much; but the surfeit of the rich will not let them sleep."*
> *Ecclesiastes 5:12*

31 Days of Winning

Saftey

If GOD is awake, YOU should be ASLEEP.

Never let your challenges and hard things keep you from resting.

Challenges are beneficial for building your character and your wealth of experiences.

God watches over and protects us from the trouble and danger we can't see.

Make wise decisions and allow God to give you safety.

31 Days of Winning

Reflection

Action

Safety

"He who keeps Israel will neither slumber nor sleep."
Psalm 121:4

31 Days of Winning

Freedom from Worry

God is bigger than deadlines.

God is bigger than missed opportunities.

God is bigger than our propensity to overcommit.

Since God is so much bigger than all of this, no adversary can overtake us.

God created the world in Genesis and the darkness could not overtake God's light. If darkness is subject to God, what makes you think problems are not?

Free yourself from worry.

Do what you can. Change what you can and allow God to settle the unsettled matters in your life.

Freedom from Worry

Reflection

Action

"But now the Lord my God has given me rest on every side; there is neither adversary nor misfortune."
1 Kings 5:4

Time Management

Your time is valuable. Don't waste it.

Set attainable goals and create a plan to reach them.

When you've done everything you can, add it to your list for tomorrow.

You are no good to anyone when you are tired and overcommitted.

Winning is about knowing your limitations, owning them, and saying NO!

Learning the art of "NO" will bless your life.
Saying NO will grant you sweet rest.

Get eight hours of sleep and start all over again tomorrow. Your body will thank you later.

Time Management

Reflection

Action

"He said, 'My presence will go with you, and I will give you rest.'"
Exodus 33:14

Reaching Out

It's great to amass wealth for yourself, but who will you help to win?

Winning requires reaching out to help others.

Who are you mentoring to be you in the next fifteen years?

Who will take your place when you are gone?

That is what it means to win and be legendary.

What we do for others, shows how full we genuinely are. Full, as in good works, good intentions, and good vibes.

Reach out and watch your legacy grow.

Reaching Out

Reflection

Action

"And the king will answer them, 'Truly I tell you, just as you did it to one of the least of these who are members of my family, you did it to me.'"
Matthew 25:40

Moving Forward

Everything begins and ends.

Some things were only meant to be temporary, while other things are meant to last forever.

Learn how to live with endings. You'll meet them over and over again. Find your focal point and stretch toward it with all your might. You'll need it.

Moving forward after hard things is especially hard, but the winner in you cannot quit.

Keep thinking. Keep planning.

Keep pursuing and stay resolute in knowing God is

rooting for your rise and plotting the next steps of your journey.

Moving Forward

Reflection

_____
_____
_____
_____
_____
_____
_____
_____
_____
_____
_____

Action

_____
_____
_____
_____
_____
_____
_____
_____
_____
_____
_____
_____

"Not that I have already obtained this or have already reached the goal; but I press on to make it my own, because Christ Jesus has made me his own."
Philippians 3:12

Weakness is Strength

Transparency and vulnerability are signs of strength, not weakness.

Who are your accountability partners? Confession is good for the soul.

Our truthtellers and cheerleaders are essential to our growth.

Surround yourself with people who will stand with you and challenge you to be the best version of you.

Friends who support you are more valuable than gold.

Be kind to them and watch your life and your spirit grow.

Weakness is Strength

Reflection

Action

> "Therefore confess your sins to one another, and pray for one another, so that you may be healed. The prayer of the righteous is powerful and effective."
> James 5:16

Speak Life

As we seek to be encouraged, remember to encourage others.

Good seeds always grow into trees of righteousness and provision. The kindness you sow today becomes the grace you reap tomorrow.

Seize every opportunity to speak life and lift the hearts of those who are broken.

How can you win if others around you are losing?

Help them win. You don't have to dim anyone else's light for your light to shine.

We can win together.

Speeak Life

Reflection

Action

"Therefore encourage one another and build up each other, as indeed you are doing."
1 Thessalonians 5:11

Have Faith

In a post-church era, it is important to remember that faith still has value for all things.

By faith, I mean faith in God.

Faith in God opens the door for God's power to be operative in our lives.

Our faith fuels our fight. When our faith is strong, our fears are weak.

Get in a Bible-teaching church. Join a small group where you can talk about Biblical truths with others. This is how you grow. Have faith.

31 Days of Winning

Reflection

_____
_____
_____
_____
_____
_____
_____
_____
_____
_____
_____
_____

Action

_____
_____
_____
_____
_____
_____
_____
_____
_____
_____
_____
_____

Have Faith

"For I am not ashamed of the gospel; it is the power of God for salvation to everyone who has faith, to the Jew first and also to the Greek. 17 For in it the righteousness of God is revealed through faith for faith; as it is written, "The one who is righteous will live by faith.""
Romans 1:16-17

31 Days of Winning

Grow

Your endurance produces character.

The more challenges you overcome, the higher your confidence rises.

Confidence is a part of your power.

You were meant to walk in authority and strength.

Hard things are a part of the growth process.

Embrace challenges when they come.

They keep you alert and prepare you for greater success.

31 Days of Winning

Reflection

_____
_____
_____
_____
_____
_____
_____
_____
_____
_____
_____

Action

_____
_____
_____
_____
_____
_____
_____
_____
_____
_____
_____

"And not only that, but we also boast in our sufferings, knowing that suffering produces endurance, and endurance produces character, and character produces hope."
Romans 5:3-4

31 Days of Winning

Stay Alert

There are energy snatchers and time wasters all around us.

Pay attention to your surroundings and be the first to identify cycles and circles.

Your rise depends on it.

The more alert you are, the more fortified you become. Sharpen your skills. Get every educational resource available to you, and create a niche-based career and consciousness.

When you do what you love, you'll always love what you're doing.

Attend to your present and your future.

Stay Alert

Reflection

Action

*"Truly the eye of the Lord is on those who fear him,
on those who hope in his steadfast love."*
Psalm 33:18

Patience

Waiting is a part of life. We wait for progress.

We wait for food at restaurants.

We wait for partners. We wait for miracles.

We wait for our own healing and renewal.

Patience is a virtue we all need.

Think of ways today that you can become more patient with others, with God, and with yourself. The patience you extend to others may be the patience you need extended to you.

31 Days of Winning

Reflection

Action

Patience

"And now, O Lord, what do I wait for? My hope is in you."
Psalm 39:7

31 Days of Winning

Hope

God is helping you and teaching how to rise and win all the time.

You are never without hope and protection. Trust God with your heart.

Trust God with your sadness, and trust God with your joy.

Hope is a gift that God gives us.

It helps us weather any storm and rise above any flaw.

You are equipped to meet the challenges of the day. Arm yourself with hope.

31 Days of Winning

Reflection

Action

Hope

"Why are you cast down, O my soul, and why are you disquieted within me? Hope in God; for I shall again praise him, my help."
Psalm 42:5

31 Days of Winning

Look Up!

You are a daughter of encouragement.

Your fight and your life help encourage others to win and pursue their futures with tenacity.

Keep looking up when discouragement tries to overtake you.

God is there, and our families, friends, loved ones, and support systems, are there cheering us on and saying fight on.

Reflection

Action

Look Up!

"There was a Levite, a native of Cyprus, Joseph, to whom the apostles gave the name Barnabas (which means son of encouragement)."
Acts 4:36

31 Days of Winning

Insecure

When life gets crazy and you feel surrounded, find solace in knowing God is with you, and you're in the space you're in on purpose.

God doesn't make mistakes.

Your insecurities disappear when you realize just how protected you are.

You are enough.

Your gifts and your talents will make room for you and place you among great men and women. The blessings are just quiet indicators that you have the DNA of a winner.

31 Days of Winning

Reflection

_____

Action

Insecure

"But let all who take refuge in you rejoice; let them ever sing for joy. Spread your protection over them, so that those who love your name may exult in you. I hide daily in His peace and provision."
Psalm 5:11

31 Days of Winning

Feed Your Spirit

The scriptures are designed to encourage us.

There are stories in the Bible for every life space and life stage. The Bible is meant to be read, but it also reads us.

Your spirit gets weak and starved by the pessimism and predictability of the world.

Feed your spirit!

Take time to read the words of Scriptures.

In these words, you will find life.

31 Days of Winning

Reflection

_____
_____
_____
_____
_____
_____
_____
_____
_____
_____
_____

Action

_____
_____
_____
_____
_____
_____
_____
_____
_____
_____
_____
_____

Feed Your Spirit

"For whatever was written in former days was written for our instruction, so that by steadfastness and by the encouragement of the scriptures we might have hope."
Romans 15:4

31 Days of Winning

Silence

God controls the elements, both wind, water, and heat. Since God can control the elements, trust God is in control of your life.

Things may not be easy, but your times are in God's hand. Being still is not a sign of futility or stagnation.

Sometimes we are still, so that we can hear God better above the noise of life.

Pause and find clarity in the silence of meditation. Quiet your thoughts so that you can hear God more clearly today.

31 Days of Winning

Reflection

Action

Silence

"Therefore we will not fear, though the earth should change, though the mountains shake in the heart of the sea."
Psalm 46:2

31 Days of Winning

Remember Who You Are

Lift your head!

Do you know who you are?

You are a child of God. That means God has you covered.

Rejoice in knowing you are a child of the King. God is for you, and God walks with you.

No request in your prayer **journey**, is too extreme. God is making provision for you right now.

Embrace God's peace, love, and power.

31 Days of Winning

Reflection

___

Action

___

Remember Who You Are

"Now my head is lifted up above my enemies all around me, and I will offer in his tent sacrifices with shouts of joy; I will sing and make melody to the Lord."
Psalm 27:6

31 Days of Winning

Seek Wisdom

Advice is invaluable, when it comes from pure hearts and sober minds.

Everyone is not meant to speak into your life.

Some voices are designed to drown out the sound of your faith, with the noise of their unbelief.

Press your ear to God's mouth.

Seek wise counsel from people who have achieved obvious success in your fields of interest.

Trust those who have been where you are going.

Pray today for wisdom and discernment today and embrace the strength of wisdom.

Seek Wisdom

Reflection

_____
_____
_____
_____
_____
_____
_____
_____
_____
_____

Action

_____
_____
_____
_____
_____
_____
_____
_____
_____
_____
_____

"Where there is no guidance, a nation falls, but in an abundance of counselors there is safety."
Proverbs 11:14

Stay Away From Negativity

Stay away from the drama! It's a distraction.

Seek ways to do good things and gravitate towards positive people.

Negative voices tend to speak against your vision, because they haven't seen what you see.

Encourage and support others, but know how to decipher opinion from facts.

Trust me, there you will find indescribable peace.

Reflection

Action

Stay Away From Negativiety

"Depart from evil, and do good; seek peace, and pursue it."
Psalm 34:14

31 Days of Winning

Joy

Joy can be found in simple things, like taking a different route to work, but arriving on time.

What about taking yourself out to lunch at a spot where you feel both empowered and creative?

These are simple actions we can repeat weekly, daily, or even monthly to infuse a sense of excitement and joy into our lives.

Working and being all things to all people can be exhausting and boring.

Wake things up! Be spontaneous. Your inner winner will thank you for it later.

Reflection

Action

Joy

*"Then I will go to the altar of God, to God my
exceeding joy; and I will praise you with the harp,
O God, my God."*
Psalm 43:4

31 Days of Winning

Trust

God has ALL power.

Trust God to lead and steer your life's path. His power overcomes fear, instability, and uncertainty.

Doubt and fear will make an occasional appearance on your life's stage, but resolve to show up and be seen.

The world is waiting for your rise. Don't trust your gifts, talents or your will.

Trust God and see your life become more meaningfully filled.

31 Days of Winning

Reflection

Action

Trust

*"Your right hand, O Lord, glorious in power— your
right hand, O Lord, shattered the enemy."
Exodus 15:6*

31 Days of Winning

Refill, Please

The Word of God is a sword that defends our heart when our soul is under siege. The more we spend in prayer and meditation, the more mindful we become.

If you feel weak or tired today, repeat the practice of filling your own well. It's good to support others, but learn how to prioritize your health and wellness.

What are you eating? Does your physical diet support the changes in your body you want to see?

In the same way, does your spiritual intake support the type of strength you want to possess in your relationship with God?

Refill yourself today and watch your light and your life grow.

Refill, Please

Reflection

Action

*"Great peace have those who love your law;
nothing can make them stumble."*
Psalm 119:165

Fuel Your Fight

People are not your adversaries, but your responses and your headspace are.

People will treat you unfairly.

They will hurt you and try to mute your authenticity.

They should not be your focus.

Their problem is likely within themselves and not with you.

Perform a spirit check today. No weapon formed against us shall prosper. God is on your side.

Reflection

Action

Fuel Your Fight

"With the Lord on my side I do not fear. What can mortals do to me?"
Psalm 118:6

31 Days of Winning

Be Amazing

You are a masterpiece. God is completing a splendid work in you.

Count your blessings.

When you walk in confidence, nothing can bring you down. Hold your head up and fear no one and nothing.

The worst-case scenario is that you don't try.

Keep evolving.

Keep being amazing.

Keep living beyond your pain and your problems.

Things always get better after a storm.

Trust God for better health and complete wholeness in your life.

Know that after this day, you've been empowered to win.

GOD IS GOING TO FINISH WHAT GOD HAS STARTED IN YOU.

Read and reread this journal until you believe it with unshakeable confidence.

Be Amazing

Reflection

Action

"I am confident of this, that the one who began a good work among you will bring it to completion by the day of Jesus Christ."
Philippians 1:6

About the Author

Jennifer L. Carner is a licensed and ordained Pastor.

She is also a renowned preacher, professor, thought-leader, mentor, and teacher.

About the Author

She has enormous depth and wisdom, cultivated over a 20+ year career in church leadership and secular education.

She enjoys spreading pearls of wisdom and positivity.

She spreads joy to all who will listen.

Jay has earned a Master of Divinity degree from the Candler School of Theology at Emory University in Atlanta, GA, and she worked for several years, teaching Epistemology, at Barry University in Tampa, Florida.

She plans to complete doctoral work in Sacred Rhetoric.

In addition to a wealth of personal honors and accomplishments, Jay has a passion for seeing others rise and achieve complete success and wholeness in their lives.

She loves bringing out the best in others and seeing everyone win. This ethos is embodied in all her work.

It is her prayer that you are both blessed and empowered by the winning woman's devotional and journal.

https://www.jennifercarnerministries.com/